1000

First Words
in Spanish

Learning Spanish

Learning a new language is fun. The best way to learn Spanish is to go to a country where it is spoken all around you. Talking with someone who knows the language very well is good, too. If possible, share this book with a grown-up who will help you to pronounce the words properly and ask you the questions under each picture.

Spanish is not a difficult language to learn but you will notice some things about it that are different from English.

In English, there is only one word for **the**. We say **the house** and **the hat**. In Spanish, there are two different words – **la casa** and **el sombrero**. If you are talking about more than one thing, instead of **the houses** and **the hats**, you say **las casas** and **los sombreros**. Each time you learn a new word in Spanish, try to learn the word for **the** that goes with it.

In the same way, **a house** and **a hat** are **una casa** and **un sombrero**. **Some houses** and **some hats** are **unas casas** and **unos sombreros**.

You may also notice that some Spanish words have little signs above the letters. These help you to pronounce the word in the right way.

Have fun learning Spanish!

1000

First Words in Spanish

Written by Nicola Baxter and Sam Budds

Illustrated by Susie Lacome

ARMADILLO

Published by Armadillo Books
an imprint of
Bookmart Limited
Registered Number 2372865
Trading as Bookmart Limited
Desford Road
Enderby
Leicester
LE9 5AD

ISBN 1 90046 683 X

Produced for Bookmart Limited by Nicola Baxter
PO Box 215
Framingham Earl
Norwich
NR14 7UR

Editorial consultant: Ronne Randall
Designer: Amanda Hawkes

Printed in Indonesia

Índice

En Casa

el cubo de basura

el cubo

la caja de herramientas

la jardinera de ventana

el tejado

el caño

la senda

la chimenea

la escalera

la ventana

la puerta

Who is in the garage?
Is the bucket blue?
Can you see two gloves?
Where are Teddy Bear's boots?

6

la radio el umbral el termo la caja de comida los ladrillos la teja la espaldera

la luz de seguridad

la calzada

el timbre

la servilleta

el aéreo

el guante

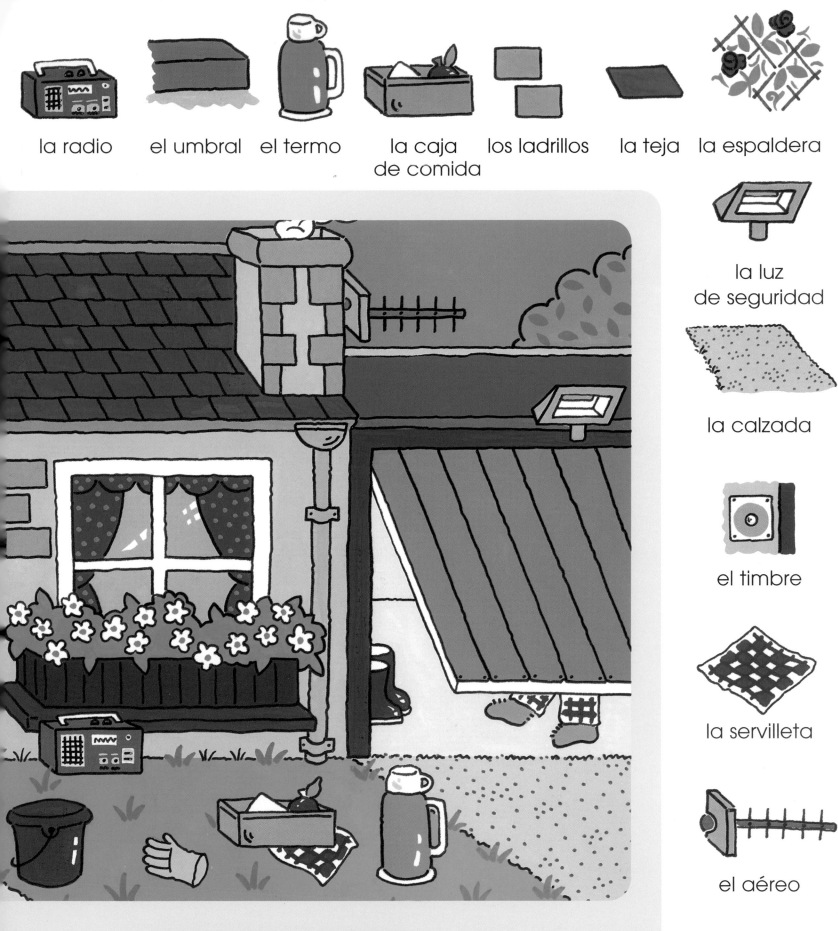

¿Quién está en el garaje?
¿Es el cubo azul?
¿Puedes ver dos guantes?
¿Dónde están las botas del Osito?

La Cocina

el jarro   la cacerola   el libro
de cocina   el tostador

el rodillo
de cocina

el tarro

el frigorífico

la cuchara
de palo

el sartén

el trapo de
cocina

la micro-onda

What is on the worktop?
Can you see the saucepan lid?
Who is looking in the fridge?
What could you use for mixing?

la tabla   el taburete   la cocina
eléctrica   el calentador
de agua   la plancha   el fregadero   la mezcladora

el jabón
de fregar

el cajón

el tablón
de anuncios

el lavaplatos

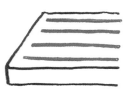

el escurreplatos

la escudilla

¿Qué hay en la tabla?
¿Puedes ver la cobertera del sartén?
¿Quién está mirando en el frigorífico?
¿Qué usas para mezclar?

El Dormitorio

el cepillo

la colcha

el pendiente

el peine

la cama

el armario

la cómoda

la mesita de noche

el pijama

el batín

la almohada

What can you see in Teddy Bear's bedroom?
What is under the bedside table?
What colour are Teddy Bear's pyjamas?
What is on the bedside table?

las zapatillas   los calcetines   el baúl   el póster   la cometa   el tebeo   la luz

la tabla de estatura

la papelera

el reloj

el dibujo

la percha

¿Qué hay en el dormitorio del Osito?
¿Qué hay debajo de la mesita?
¿De qué color es el pijama del Osito?
¿Qué hay en la mesita?

la hucha

11

El Cuarto de Baño

el jabón   el paño   la esponja   el cepillo de dientes

el baño

el lavabo

el papel higiénico

la ducha

la cortina de ducha

la estera de baño

el armario

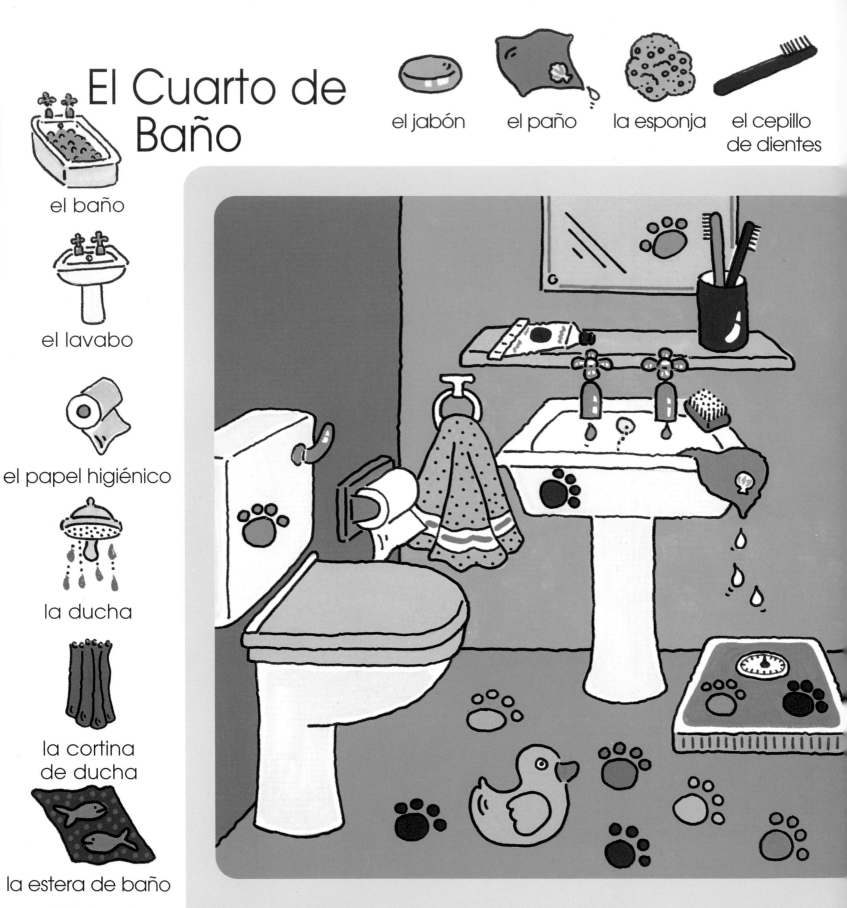

What colour are the wall tiles?
What is on the bath mat?
How many toothbrushes can you see?
How many pawprints can you find?

 el váter

 el espejo

 el cepillo

 el grifo

 la balanza

 la toalla

 el champú

 el jabón de baño

 la pasta de dientes

 el barco

 los azulejos

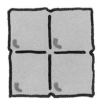 el cepillo de espalda

 el pato

¿De qué color son los azulejos?
¿Qué hay en la estera de baño?
¿Cuántos cepillos de dientes hay?
¿Cuántas huellas de patas hay?

El Salón

el reloj

la cortina la lámpara

el cojín

la alfombra

la butaca

la estantería

la revista

el aspirador

la planta

el trapo de polvo

What is on the sofa?
How many dusters can you see?
What is on the bookcase?
What colour is the armchair?

14

| el periódico | el vaso de flores | el vídeo | la foto | la maqueta | la obra | la mesa |

el tele control

el sofá

la chimenea

la televisión

el estéreo

¿Qué hay en la sofá?
¿Cuántos trapos de polvo hay?
¿Qué hay en la estantería?
¿De qué color es la butaca?

el papel
de paredes

El Desván

la cuna   la casa de muñecas   la jaula   el tragaiuz

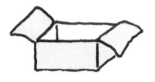

el cartón

el cuadro

la maleta

el maniquí

el patín

la bombilla

la telaraña

How many jamjars can you see?
What is on the sledge?
Can you see a bed?
What is red and white?

16

el bote de pintura

la tumbona

las botellas

el sombrero de paja

los tarros

la escotilla

la caña

la mecedora

los adornos

la máquina de coser

el caballo de balancín

los botes del patinaje

el trineo

¿Cuántos tarros hay?
¿Qué hay sobre el trineo?
¿Puedes ver una cama?
¿Qué hay de rojo y blanco?

El Jardín

la carretilla

las tijeras
de jardín

la tierra

la pala

la maceta

la regadera

la manga

la horca

la césped

el
cortacesped

las semillas

What is on the grass?
What is in the wheelbarrow?
How many birds can you see?
What colour is the watering can?

los hojas

el nido

la azada

la horca del mano

la paleta

la mesita de pájaros

el cobertizo

la cesta de plantas

el rastrillo

el seto

las flores

el baño de pájaros

la escoba

¿Qué hay sobre la césped?
¿Qué hay en la caretilla?
¿Cuántos pájaros hay?
¿De qué color es la regadera?

19

La Calle

 la bicicleta la paloma los caramelos  el pastel

la acera

la verja

la farola

la papelera

la furgoneta

el conductor

la silleta

How many wheels can you see?
Which shop sells lollipops?
What colour are the boots in the shoe shop?
Do you like cakes?

20

el colegio la panadería el paquete la calle el piruí la boca de alcantarilla el casco

la bolsa

la zapatería

el poste indicador

la bombonería

la cuerda de saltar

las botas

¿Cuántas ruedas hay?
¿Cuál de las tiendas venden los pirulís?
¿De qué color son las botas en la zapatería?
¿A ti, te gusta los pasteles?

El Supermercado

 el monedero

 el dinero la fruta

 el bolso

las latas

el comprador

el carro

la cola

la cesta

la bolsa

la caja

How many bears are in the queue?
Can you see Teddy Bear?
Where is the milk?
What is on the conveyor belt?

la leche

 las llaves

 el yogur

 el cartón

 el zumo

 la miel

 el código

 la dependienta

 el recibo

 el signo

 el cajero

 los legumbres

 la cinta transportadora

¿Cuántos osos están en la cola?
¿Puedes ver el Osito?
¿Dónde está la leche?
¿Qué hay en la cinta transportadora?

23

La Escuela

 la profesora

 los rotuladores

 el papel

 el tarro de agua

 la regla

 la pizarra

 el mapa

 los coloretes

 la arcilla

la tiza

 la percha

What is the teacher holding?
What do you need for painting?
How many pupils can you see?
What colour is the ruler?

24

el alumno el pincel la goma el dibujo la pecera el cabellete las pinturas

el alfabeto

el cuaderno

el ordenador

el bolso

el rompecabezas

¿Qué hay en la mano de la profesora?
¿Qué necesitas para hacer la pintura?
¿Cuántos alumnos hay?
¿De qué color es la regla?

las tijeras

El Transporte

el helicoptero

el globo

el cohete

el paracaída

el autocár

el coche

el camión de averías

la caravana

el carro

el coche clásico

el tándem

la escavadora

Can you see Teddy Bear?
What colour is the refuse truck?
Which car is very old?
How many cars can you see?

el coche de carreras

la apisonadora

el furgón de basura

el camión

el gokart

la furgoneta

la moto

el camión de gasolina

la escavadora

la transportadora de coches

el furgón

¿Dónde está el Osito?
¿De qué color es el furgón de basura?
¿Cuál de los coches es muy viejo?
¿Cuántos coches hay?

La Granja

la cordera   la oveja   el cerdo   el cerdito

los pollitos

la gallina

el perro

el caballo

el potro

el granjero

la granja

Where is the duck?
What is the farmer holding?
How many chicks does he have?
Is the tractor yellow?

28

el pato

el patito

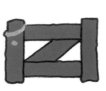

el gato

la rata

la puerta
de verja

la valla

el espanta
pájaros

el estanque

el gallo

la vaca

el ternero

el campo

¿Dónde está la pata?
¿Qué lleva el granjero?
¿Cuántos pollitos hay?
¿Es amarillo, el tractór?

el tractór

29

El Parque

el helado

el tobogán

los columpios

el corredor

el hoyo de arena

la fuente

el macizo de flores

el banco

la rodillera

el pájaro

la sirena

Is Teddy Bear on the swing?
What is in the hamper?
How many bears are wearing helmets?
How many wheels does a tricycle have?

el triciclo

el monopatín

el subibaja

las ruedas

el cesto

el arco

la pelota

el picnic

la ardilla

los bocadillos

el patinete

los pátines

el estereo personal

¿Está el Osito en el columpios?
¿Qué hay en el cesto?
¿Cuántos de los osos llevan los cascos?
¿Cuántas ruedas tienen el triciclo?

El Mundo de Libros

la varilla de virtudes

el fuente
de deseos

el hongo

el elfo

el hada

la lanza

el escudo

la corona

la espada

la armadura

el dragón

el caballero   la princesa

Who can do magic?
What colour is the dragon?
Where does a king live?
Who wears armour?

la bandana

el sombrero de copa

el paje

la calabaza

el mágico

el príncipe

la reina

el rey

la capa

el gigante

el castillo

¿Quién hace el mágico?
¿De qué color es el dragón?
¿Dónde vive el rey?
¿Quién lleva la armadura?

El Campo

las tiendas de campaña el árbol el paseante el puente

el bosque

la montaña

el campo

el río

el lago

la rama

la hoguera

How many carriages does the engine have?
Who is sitting on a log?
Is the sleeping bag in the tent?
Is the rowing boat on the river?

34

el tronco   el tren   el vagón   el arbusto   los gemelos   la cascada   los troncos

el pueblo

la vía

el bote de remos

la colina

el saco de dormir

las rocas

¿Cuántos vagones tienen el tren?
¿Quién está sentado en los troncos?
¿Está en la tienda, el saco de dormir?
¿Está en el río , el bote de remos?

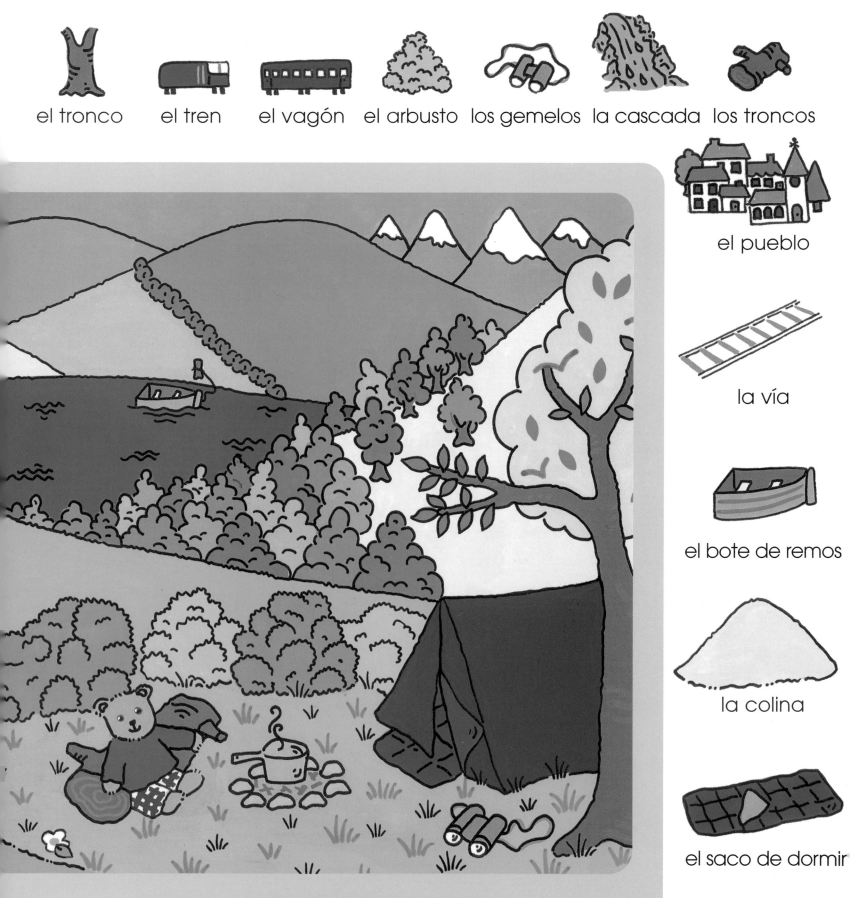

El Puerto

la pez   el canalete   la cuerda   la boya

la portilla

el submarino

el transatlántico

el pescador

la grúa

el pescadero

el barco
de motor

What can go under the water?
What are round windows on a boat called?
How many fish can you see?
What is on the jetty?

el chaleco
salvavidas   el gancho   la áncora   la langosta   el mástil   la canoa   el esquiador
acuático

la langostera

el traje de baño

el embarcadero

el buque

el saltador

la guindola

¿Qué va debajo del mar?
¿Cómo se llama las ventanas redondas de un barco?
¿Cuántos peces hay?
¿Qué hay en el embarcadero?

El Aeropuerto

los servicios   el hangar   la etiqueta   el tablón

el bastón

el batido

el caro

las llegadas

el autobús

el avión

la torre
de control

How many suitcases can you see?
Who is carrying a mop?
Can you see our Teddy Bear?
Have you ever flown in an aeroplane?

| la maleta | el café | la pista de aterrizaje | el fregasuelos | la limpiadora | los billetes | la máquina de fotos |

la mango

el piloto

el puente de control

la azafata

la mochila

el teléfono

¿Cuántas maletas hay?
¿Quién lleva un fregasuelos?
¿Dónde está nuestro Osito?
¿Has viajado en un avión?

39

El Hospital

 la bandeja

 la enfermera

 el vaso de agua

 la venda

 la sabana

 el médico

 el camisón

 la medicina

 el visitante

 las muletas

 el algodón

What is the nurse holding?
Who is in the lift?
Is the doctor's coat red?
Have you ever been in hospital?

el ascensor

 el portero

 el reloj

 el cabestrillo

 la tirita

la jeringa

 la manta

 la tarjeta

 la escayola

 la tabla de temperatura

el estetoscopio

 el termómetro

 la silla de ruedas

¿Qué tiene la enfermera?
¿Quién está en el ascensor?
¿Es rojo, la chaqueta del médico?
¿Has estado una vez en el hospital?

41

El Mar

la bandera de pirata

el caballito de mar

la cadena

la perla

la ballena

el galeón

el mensaje de botella

el tiburón

el nadador

el cajón

la medusa

What is on the island?
What is in the sea?
What goes in a keyhole?
Which is the biggest animal in the sea?

 el coral

 el pulpo

 el pirata

 el delfín

 la pistola

 el pedazo del ojo

 la ostra

 la mapa

 el agujero de llave

 la isla

 las algas

 la sirena

la palmera

¿Qué hay en la isla?
¿Qué hay en el mar?
¿Qué va en el agujero de llave?
En el mar, ¿cuál es el animal más grande?

La Juguetería

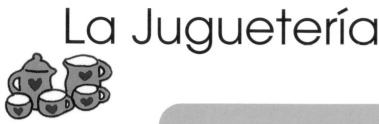

 el ábaco

 el juego
de bolos

 el castillo

 la muñeca

el servicio de té

la caja sorpresa

las pinturas

la peonza

la casa
de muñecas

el juego

el títere

How many building bricks can you see?
Who is holding a glove puppet?
Which toys are for babies?
Which is your favourite toy?

el collar   la caretilla   el yoyo   los dados   las carnicas   el robot   las tazitas

los cubos

la jugueta
de bébés

los solditos

el libro de colores

el coche

la disfraz

¿Cuántos cubos hay?

¿Quién lleva un títere?

¿Cuáles de los juguetes son para los bébés?

¿Cuál es tú juguete preferido?

45

El Taller

la llave
de tuercas

la lámpara
de bolsillo

la taza

el taladero

el bolsillo

el calendario

el estante

el pomo
de puerta

el metro

las galletas

la Arca de Noé

How many animals can you see?
What is on the workbench?
What is on the shelf?
What colour is the door?

la sierra   el destornillador   los tornillos   los clavos   el martillo   los anteojos   la navaja

el papel de lija

el mazo

el tablón

los animales

los alicates

la mesa de trabajo

¿Cuántos animales hay?
¿Qué hay en la mesa de trabajo?
¿Qué hay en el estante?
¿De qué color es la puerta?

47

La Playa

la bandera   la arena   la concha de mar   el mar

el castillo de arena

la estrella de mar

el bañador

la sombrilla

las pierdrecitas

la red

las gafas de sol

How many legs does a starfish have?
How many sea shells can you see?
What is very cold?
What colour is the flag?

48

 el cangrejo

 las aletas

 el barco de yate

 los brazales

 el sol

 las olas

 la crema bronceadora

 el faro

 el aro de goma

 la pelota

 el traje de baño

 la gaviota

 el helado

¿Cuántos brazos tiene la estrella de mar?
¿Cuántas conchas hay?
¿Hay algo que es muy frío?
¿De qué color es la bandera?

La Fiesta

el regalo

el payaso

la vela

el botón

la pajita

el sombrero
de fiesta

la ración
de la tarta

la gaseosa

la taza de papel

el mantel

la tarta

How old is the birthday bear?
How old are you?
How many balloons can you see?
Who is under the table?

50

el chaleco   la cinta   el globo   la corbata de lazo   la máscara   el lazo   la venda

el papel

la guirnalda de papel

el bolsito de fiesta

el sobre

la tarjeta

el vestido

¿Cuántos años tiene el osito?
¿Cuántos años tienes tú?
¿Cuántos globos hay?
¿Quién etsá debajo de la mesa?

El Cuerpo

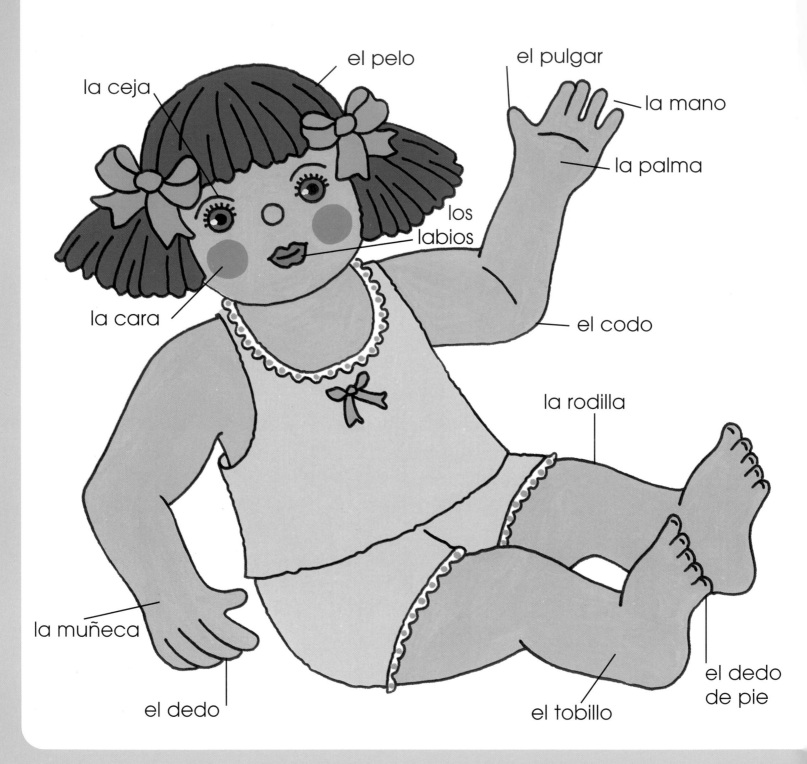

el pelo

la ceja

el pulgar

la mano

la palma

los labios

la cara

el codo

la rodilla

la muñeca

el dedo

el tobillo

el dedo de pie

How many toes does Dolly have?
What colour is her hair?
Do you have paws?
Are your eyes blue like Teddy's?

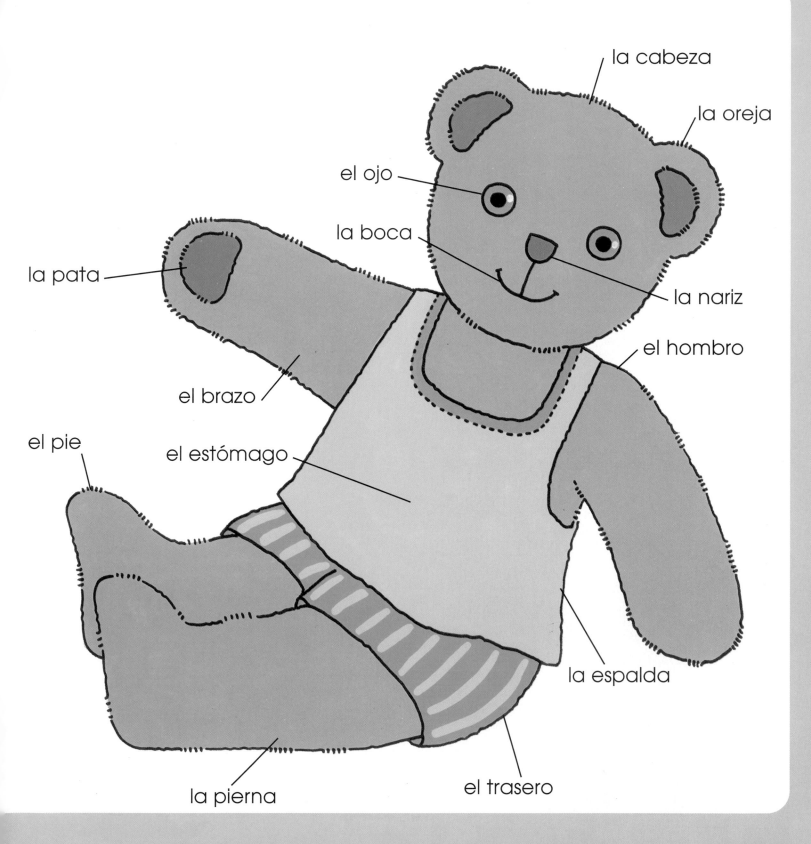

la cabeza

la oreja

el ojo

la boca

la nariz

la pata

el hombro

el brazo

el pie

el estómago

la espalda

la pierna

el trasero

¿Cuántos dedos de pie tiene la muñeca?
¿De qué color es su pelo?
¿Tienes patas?
¿Tienes los ojos azules como el Osito?

Haciendo Cosas

gatear

sentar

leer

abrazar

cantar

beber

comer

escribir

agitar el brazo

lavarse

secarse

dormir

What do you like to do?
What is Teddy Bear doing?
What do babies like doing?
Are you sitting or standing?

dar un puntapié

saltar

montar la bicicleta

saltar

andar

poner la ropa

correr

saltar

empujar

tirar

bailar

esperar

¿Qué te gusta hacer?
¿Qué hace el Osito?
¿Qué les gustan hacer los bébés?
¿Estás sentado o levantado?

Las Estaciones

la primervera

el verano

el otoño

el invierno

Which season is it now?
Is there snow in the summer?
When does Teddy Bear fly his kite?
What comes from clouds?

El Tiempo

 el sol

 la nieve

 el arco de iris

 el helado

 el ventarrón

 los carámbanos

 el viento

 el copo de nieve

 el nube

 el tornado

 el hombre de nieve

la lluvia

el rocío

 el relámpago

 el

 la inundación

la helada

la niebla

 el frío

 los charcos

¿En qué estación del año estamos ahora?
¿Hay nieve en el verano?
¿Cuándo lanza su cometa, el Osito?
¿Qué viene de los nubes?

La Comida Preferida

la mantequilla

la galleta

los cereales

el azúcar

la sopa

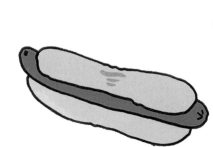
el perrito caliente

las patatas fritas

la salsa

el chocolate

el arroz

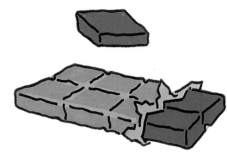
los churros

los espaguetis

What is your favourite food?
Do you like cheese?
How many spoons can you see?
What is on Teddy Bear's ears?

la ensalada

la hamburguesa

la pizza

las judías asadas

el pastel

el queso

el pan

la salchicha

las nueces

la harina

la tortilla

la tarta

¿Cuál es tu comida preferida?
¿A ti, te gusta el queso?
¿Cuántas cucharas hay?
¿Qué hay en las orejas del Osito?

Los Deportes

el criquet

el béisbol

el fútbol americano

el tenis

la salta alta

el tiro con arco

la carrera de tres piernas

la escaleda

la natación

el salto con pértiga

el equipo

la gimnasia

Can you see Teddy Bear?
Which sports need a ball?
Which is your favourite sport?
How many bears are waving?

el salto de
trampolín

el ciclismo

el levantamiento
de pesos

el piragüismo

el patinaje
de ruedas

el golf

el fútbol

la carrera
de bolsas

el patinaje

el baloncesto

el judo

la copa

¿Puedes ver el Osito?
¿Cuál de los deportes necesitan una pelota?
¿Cuál es tu deporte preferido?
¿Cuántos de los osos están agitando los brazos?

La Música

la pandereta

el tríangulo

los platillos

las maracas

el violín

el teclado de música

el trombón

la flauta de pico

el atril

las notas

el director

el violoncelo

Can you play these instruments?
Which instruments do you blow?
Which instruments have strings?
Which instruments do you hit?

la flauta   la música   el oboe   la trompeta

el saxafón   el banjo   el xilofón   la guitarra

la harpa   el piano   los tímpanos

¿Tocas algunos de estos instrumentos?
¿Cuáles de los instrumentos soplas?
¿Cuáles de los instrumentos tienen cuerdas?
¿Cuáles de los instrumentos tienes que golpear?

Los Bébés

el sonajero el babero el biberón el chupete

las botas de lana

el monitor

el colchón de cambiante

el libro de bébé

la hucha

la camiseta de dormir

la camita

Do baby bears sleep in a big bed?
What colour is the trainer cup?
What are the baby bears wearing?
Do you have a money box?

64

el cochecito

el chal

el pañal

el tisú

el chupador

el orinal

la silla alta

la tazita

el libro de tela

el libro de cartón

el juguete mimosa

el colchón

¿Duermen en una cama grande los ositos?
¿De qué color es la tazita?
¿Qué llevan los ositos?
¿Tienes una hucha?

el bolso de bébés

Los Números

una casa

dos coches

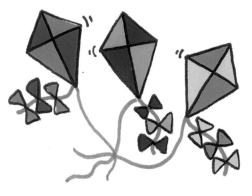
tres cometas

cuatro conéjos

cinco globos

seis patas

siete fresas

ocho coloretes

nueve flores

diez corozones

What colour are the rabbits?
How many bears can you see?
How many flowers can you count?
What is five plus seven?

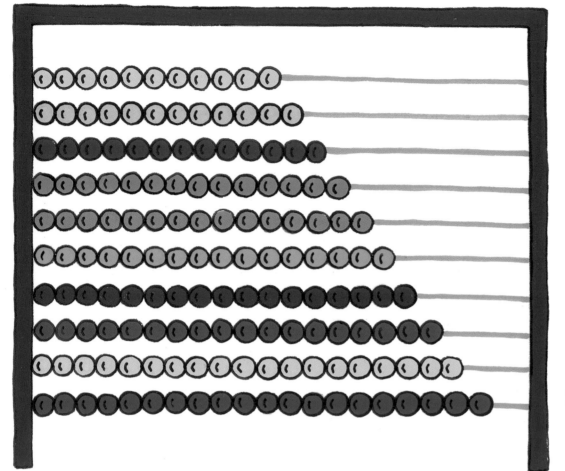

11 once

12 doce

13 trece

14 catorce

15 quince

16 dieciseis

17 diecisiete

18 dieciocho

19 diecinueve

20 veinte

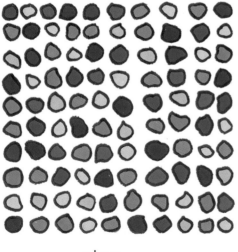

cien

tecero   segundo   primero

¿De qué color son los conejos?
¿Cuántos osos hay?
¿Cuántos flores hay?
Suma cinco y siete.

Los Colores

azul · rojo · gris · rosa · verde

blanco

negro

amarillo

marrón

violeta

naranja

azul oscurro

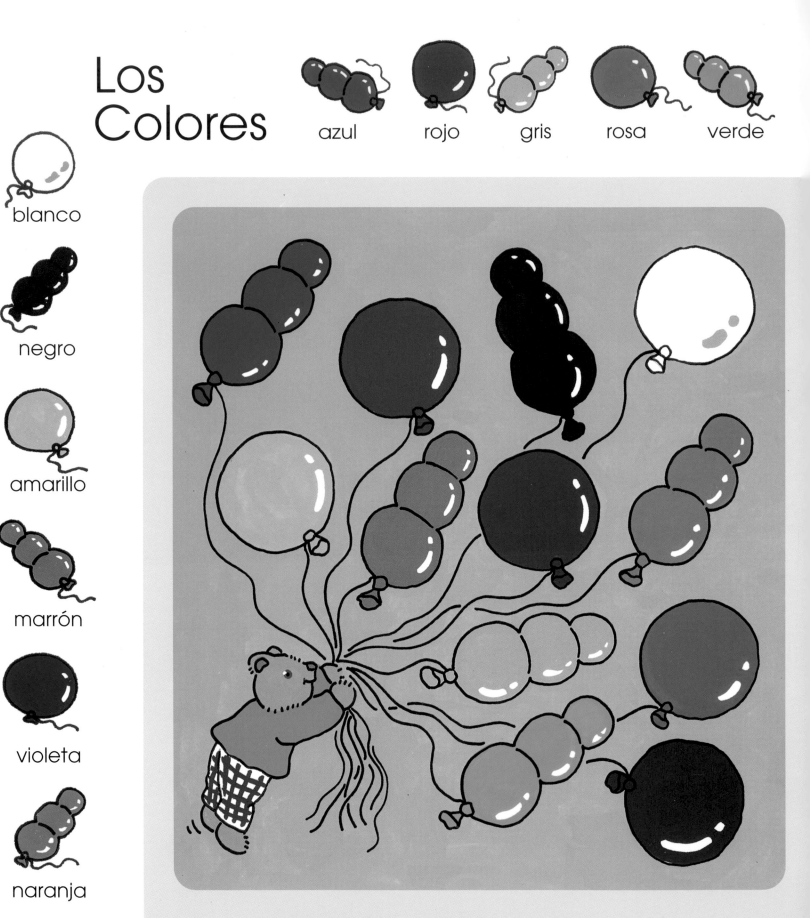

What is your favourite colour?
What colour is Teddy Bear's top?
Are there zigzags on Teddy Bear's trousers?
Which shape is pink?

Las Formas

la corazón

las rayas

el circulo

el cuadro

la estrella

el diamante

el rectangulo

los zig zag

los puntos

la ovalada

el triangulo

los cuadrados

¿Cuál es tu color preferido?
¿De qué color es el jersey del Osito?
¿Hay los zig zag en los pantalones del Osito?
¿Cuál de las formas es de color rosa?

La Ropa

el sombrero   el panuelo   los guantes   las zapatillas de deporte

la bufunda

los vaqueros

la chaqueta

la blusa

la camiseta

los pantalones

el suéter

What do you wear on a hot day?
What do you wear on a cold day?
What colour are the mittens?
What are you wearing now?

el
plumífero

las botas

los
pantalones cortes

la falda

las bragas

la
camiseta

la pinza

los zapatos

el mono

la camisa

el abrigo

la corbata

las medias

¿Qué llevas cuando hace frío?
¿Qué llevas cuando hace color?
¿De qué color son los guantes?
¿Qué llevas ahora?

71

La Familia

la bisabuela   el bisabuelo

la abuela   el abuelo   la bistía   el bistío

el padre   la madre   la tía   el tío

la hermana   el Osito   el hermano   la prima   los gemelos

Do you have any brothers or sisters?
How many brothers does Teddy Bear have?
How are you feeling now?
Are you frightened of spiders?

Los Sentimientos

asustada

contento

tímido

desconcierta

aburrido

enfadado

pensativo

triste

orgulloso

arrepentido

¿Tienes hermanos o hermanas?
¿Cuántos hermanos tiene el Osito?
¿Qué tal?
¿Tienes miedo de las arañas?

La Fruta

 la pera

 el plátano

la sandía

 la lima

la frambuesa

las uvas

el vaccinio

el higo

el mango

el ruibarbo

la uva espina

Which is your favourite fruit?
How many bananas can you see?
What is Teddy Bear holding?
Which fruits are red?

74

la naránja

el
melocotón

el limón

la ciruela

el
albaricoque

la cereza

la manzana

la papaya

el pomelo

la fresa

la grosella roja

la mandarina

la piña

¿Cuál es tu fruta preferida?
¿Cuántos plátanos hay?
¿Qué lleva el Osito?
¿Cuáles de las frutas son rojas?

75

Los Legumbres

los champiñones

la zanahoria

el brécol

el pimiento rojo

los guisantes

los puerros

la maíz

la cebolla

la patata

la coliflor

el tomate

el apio

Do you like carrots?
What is Teddy Bear eating?
Which vegetables are green?
What is your favourite vegetable?

 la lechuga

 la remolacha

 las judías

 la chirivía

 el pepino

 el rabaño

 la batata

 las judías verdes

 el nabo

 las hierbas

 la col

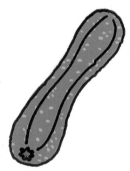 el pepinito

¿A ti, te gusta las zanahorias?
¿Qué come el Osito?
¿Cuáles de los legumbres son verdes?
¿Cuál es tu legumbre preferido?

Las Flores

 la amapola   el lirio    la magarita   la campanula

el pensamiento

la narciso

la dalia

la girasol

el clavel

la azucena

la rosa

Which flowers are yellow?
Which flower grows very tall?
What is under the cup?
What is Teddy Bear holding?

¡A Comer!

la cucharilla

el pimiento

la sal

el platillo

la taza

el plato

el cuchillo

el tenedor

la cucharilla

el salvamanteles

el vaso

el cántarro

¿Cuáles de las flores son amarillos?
¿Cuál de las flores crece muy alto?
¿Qué hay debajo de la taza?
¿Qué tiene el Osito en su mano?

Las Palabras Opuestas

lento

rápido

grande

pequeño

alto

bajo

abierto

cerrado

puesto

apagado

abajo

arriba

Is an elephant small?
Is this book open or shut?
Are you inside or outside?
Are balloons heavy?

arriba

abajo

viejo

nuevo

lleno

vacío

ligero

pesado

dentro

fuera

delgado

gordo

¿Es pequeño el elefante?
¿Es abierto o cerrado el libro?
¿Estás a dentro o a fuera?
¿Están pesados, los globos?

Las Pájaros

la pluma

el huevo

el nido

el pico

el ala

el búho

el frailecillo

el tucán

el pingüino

el pavoreal

el avestruz

el emú

What is in the nest?
How many beaks can you see?
Which birds are black and white?
Which birds are eating fishes?

el martín
pescador

la golondrina

el kiwi

el colbrí

el albatros

el buitre

la oca

el pavo

el flamenco

el pelícano

la cigüeña

el cisne

¿Qué hay en el nido?
¿Cuántos picos hay?
¿Cuáles de los pájaros son blancos y negros?
¿Cuáles de los pájaros comen el pescado?

Los Insectos
y otros animales pequeños

 la abeja
 el caracol
 la mariquita
 la lagartija

el gusano

la mariposa

la avispa

la oruga

el escarabajo

el milpiés

el camaleón

Which minibeasts have wings?
Which minibeast has six black spots?
Which minibeast carries its own house?
Which minibeasts do not have legs?

 la mariposa nocturna

 la hormiga

 el saltamontes

 la babosa

 la mosca

 la pulga

 la crisálida

 el insecto de palo

 la tarántula

 el sapo

 el ciempiés

 la libélula

 la araña

¿Cuáles de los insectos tienen las alas?

¿Cuál tiene seis puntos negros?

¿Cuál lleva su propia casa?

¿Cuáles no tienen piernas?

Los Animales

la coala   el rinoceronte   el armadillo   el canguro

el oso polar   el gorila   la jirafa   el mono

el tigre   el elefante   la serpiente   el panda

Which animal is very tall?
Which animal is very big?
Which animal is Teddy Bear feeding?
Which is your favourite animal?

el mapache   el bisonte   el puerco espín   la cebra

el oso   el cocodrilo   el camello   el león

el cobo   el leopardo   el castor   el hipopótamo

¿Cuál de los animales es muy alto?
¿Cuál de los animales es muy grande?
¿El Osito da la comida a cuál de los animales?
¿Cuál es tu animal preferido?

Los Animales Doméstitos

la casa del perro   el gatito   el hámster   la conejera

el canario

el conejo

el loro

el periquito

el conejo de indias

la comida de peces

el pez de colores

Do you have a pet?
Who lives in a kennel?
Where is the rabbit?
What is in the fish tank?

el cachorro   las burbujas   la escoba   la tortuga   el hueso   la traílla   el cuello

el tazón de perro

la cesta del gato

el tanque

la puerta de gatos

la tortuga marina

el tazón de agua

¿Tienes animales en casa?
¿Quién vive en la casa del perro?
¿Dónde está el conejo?
¿Qué hay en el tanque?

La Lista de Palabras

a

abacus   *el ábaco*
aerial   *el aéreo*
aeroplane   *el avión*
airport bus   *el autobús*
alarm clock   *el reloj*
albatross   *el albatros*
alphabet   *el alfabeto*
American football
   el fútbol americano
anchor   *la áncora*
angry   *enfadado*
animals   *los animales*
ankle   *el tobillo*
anorak   *el plumífero*
ant   *la hormiga*
apple   *la manzana*
apricot   *el*
   albaricoque
aquarium   *la pecera*
archery   *el tiro con*
   arco
arm   *el brazo*
armadillo   *el armadillo*
armbands   *los*
   brazales
armchair   *la butaca*
armour   *la armadura*
arrivals board   *las*
   llegadas
aunt   *la tía*
autumn   *el otoño*

b

baby alarm   *el*
   monitor
baby record book
   el libro de bébé
back   *la espalda*
back brush   *el cepillo*
   de espalda
baggage trolley   *el*
   caro
baked beans   *las*
   judías asadas

bakery   *la panadería*
ball   *la pelota*
balloon   *el globo*
banana   *el plátano*
bandage   *la venda*
banjo   *el banjo*
banner   *la bandana*
barcode   *el código*
baseball   *el béisbol*
basketball   *el*
   baloncesto
bath   *el baño*
bath mat   *la estera*
   de baño
beachball   *la pelota*
beads   *el collar*
beak   *el pico*
bear   *el oso*
beaver   *el castor*
bed   *la cama*
bedside table   *la*
   mesita de noche
bee   *la abeja*
beetle   *el escarabajo*
beetroot   *la*
   remolacha
bench   *el banco*
bib   *el babero*
bicycle   *la bicicleta*
big   *grande*
binoculars   *los*
   gemelos
bird   *el pájaro*
bird bath   *el baño*
   de pájaros
bird table   *la mesita*
   de pájaros
birthday cake   *la tarta*
birthday card   *la*
   tarjeta
biscuit   *la galleta*
black   *negro*
blanket   *la manta*
blindfold   *la venda*
blouse   *la blusa*
blue   *azul*

bluebell   *la*
   campanula
blueberries   *el*
   vaccinio
board book   *el libro*
   de cartón
board game   *el juego*
bone   *el hueso*
bookcase   *la*
   estantería
bootees   *las botas*
   de lana
boots   *las botas*
bored   *aburrido*
bottles   *las botellas*
bottom (body)   *el*
   trasero
bottom (position)
   abajo
bow   *el lazo*
bow tie   *la corbata*
   de lazo
branch   *la rama*
bread   *el pan*
bricks   *los ladrillos*
bridge   *el puente*
briefcase   *la maleta*
broad beans   *las*
   judías
broccoli   *el brécol*
broom   *la escoba*
brother   *el hermano*
brown   *marrón*
brush   *el cepillo*
bubble bath   *el*
   jabón de baño
bubbles   *las burbujas*
bucket   *el cubo*
budgerigar   *el*
   periquito
buffalo   *el bisonte*
buggy   *la silleta*
bulldozer   *la*
   escavadora
buoy   *la boya*
bush   *el arbusto*
butter   *la mantequilla*

butterfly   *la mariposa*
button   *el botón*

c

cabbage   *la col*
cabinet   *el armario*
cage   *la jaula*
cake   *el pastel*
calendar   *el*
   calendario
calf   *el ternero*
camel   *el camello*
camera   *la máquina*
   de fotos
camp fire   *la hoguera*
camper van   *la*
   caravana
canary   *el canario*
candle   *la vela*
canoe   *la canoa*
cans   *las latas*
car   *el coche*
car transporter   *la*
   transportadora de
   coches
caravan   *la caravana*
cardboard box   *el*
   cartón
carnation   *el clavel*
carpet   *la maqueta*
carriage   *el vagón*
carrier bag   *la bolsa*
carrot   *la zanahoria*
carton   *el cartón*
cashier   *el cajero*
castle   *el castillo*
cat   *el gato*
cat basket   *la cesta*
   del gato
cat flap   *la puerta*
   de gatos
caterpillar   *la oruga*
cauliflower   *la coliflor*
celery   *el apio*
cello   *el violoncelo*
centipede   *el*
   ciempiés

cereal   *los cereales*
chain   *la cadena*
chalk   *la tiza*
chalkboard   *la pizarra*
chameleon   *el cameleón*
changing bag   *el bolso de bébés*
changing mat   *el colchón de cambiante*
check-in desk   *el puente de control*
checks   *los cuadrados*
cheek   *la cara*
cheese   *el queso*
cherry   *la cereza*
chest of drawers   *la cómoda*
chicks   *los pollitos*
chimney   *la chimenea*
chips   *las patatas fritas*
chocolate   *el chocolate*
chrysalis   *la crisálida*
circle   *el circulo*
cleaner   *la limpiadora*
climbing (sport)   *la escaleda*
clipboard   *el tablón*
cloak   *la capa*
clock   *el reloj*
cloth book   *el libro de tela*
clothes peg   *la pinza*
cloud   *el nube*
clown   *el payaso*
coach   *el autocár*
coat   *el abrigo*
coat hook   *la percha*
coathanger   *la percha*
cockerel   *el gallo*
coffee   *el café*
cold   *el frío*
collar   *el cuello*
coloured pencils   *las pinturas*

colouring book   *el libro de colores*
comb   *el peine*
comic   *el tebeo*
computer   *el ordenador*
conductor   *el director*
container ship   *el buque*
control tower   *la torre de control*
conveyor belt   *la cinta transportadora*
cookbook   *el libro de cocina*
cookies   *las galletas*
coral   *el coral*
cot   *la camita*
cotton wool   *el algodón*
courgette   *el pepinito*
cousin   *la prima*
cow   *la vaca*
crab   *el cangrejo*
cradle   *la cuna*
crane   *la grúa*
crawling   *gatear*
crayons   *los coloretes*
cricket   *el criquet*
crocodile   *el cocodrilo*
crown   *la corona*
cucumber   *el pepino*
cuddling   *abrazar*
cuddly toy   *el juguete mimosa*
cup   *la copa*
curtain   *la cortina*
cushion   *el cojín*
cycling   *el ciclismo*
cymbals   *los platillos*

d

daffodil   *la narciso*
dahlia   *la dalia*
daisy   *la magarita*
dancing   *bailar*

deck chair   *la tumbona*
decorations   *los adornos*
delivery van   *la furgoneta*
dew   *el rocío*
diamond   *el diamante*
dice   *los dados*
digger   *la escavadora*
dishwasher   *el lava platos*
diver   *el saltador*
doctor   *el médico*
dog   *el perro*
dog bowl   *el tazón de perro*
doll   *la muñeca*
doll's house   *la casa de muñecas*
dolphin   *el delfín*
door   *la puerta*
doorbell   *el timbre*
doorknob   *el pomo de puerta*
doorstep   *el umbral*
doughnuts   *los churros*
down   *abajo*
dragon   *el dragón*
dragonfly   *la libélula*
drain   *la boca de alcantarilla*
draining board   *el escurreplatos*
drawer   *el cajón*
dressing   *poner la ropa*
dressing gown   *el batín*
dressing-up outfit   *la disfraz*
dressmaker's dummy   *el maniquí*
drill   *el taladero*
drinking straw   *la pajita*
drinking   *beber*
driver   *el conductor*
driveway   *la calzada*
drying   *secarse*

duck   *el pato*
duckling   *el patito*
dumper truck   *el carro*
dungarees   *el mono*
dustbin   *el cubo de basura*
duster   *el trapo de polvo*
duvet   *la colcha*

e

ear   *la oreja*
easel   *el caballete*
eating   *comer*
egg   *el huevo*
eight   *ocho*
eighteen   *dieciocho*
elbow   *el codo*
elephant   *el elefante*
eleven   *once*
elf   *el elfo*
embarrassed   *desconcierta*
empty   *vacío*
emu   *el emú*
engine   *el tren*
envelope   *el sobre*
eraser   *la goma*
exercise book   *el cuaderno*
eye patch   *el pedazo del ojo*
eye   *el ojo*
eyebrow   *la ceja*

f

fairy   *el hada*
farmer   *el granjero*
farmhouse   *la granja*
fast   *rápido*
fat   *gordo*
father   *el padre*
feather   *la pluma*
feeding bottle   *el biberón*
felt pens   *los rotuladores*
fence   *la valla*

field *el campo*
fifteen *quince*
fig *el higo*
finger *el dedo*
fireplace *la chimenea*
first *primero*
fish *la pez*
fish food *la comida de peces*
fish tank *el tanque*
fisherman *el pescador*
fishing boat *el barco pescadero*
fishing net *la red*
fishing rod *la caña*
five *cinco*
fizzy drink *la gaseosa*
flag *la bandera*
flamingo *el flamenco*
flannel *el paño*
flask *el termo*
flea *la pulga*
flippers *las aletas*
flood *la inundación*
flour *la harina*
flower bed *el macizo de flores*
flowerpot *la maceta*
flowers *las flores*
flute *la flauta*
fly *la mosca*
foal *el potro*
fog *la niebla*
food mixer *la mezcladora*
foot *el pie*
forest *el bosque*
fork (garden) *la horca*
fork (table) *el tenedor*
fort *el castillo*
fountain *la fuente*
four *cuatro*
fourteen *catorce*
fridge *el frigorifico*
frightened *asustada*
frog *el sapo*
frost *la helada*
fruit *la fruta*
frying pan *el sartén*

full *lleno*

g

gale *el ventarrón*
galleon *el galeón*
gate *la puerta de verja*
get-well card *la tarjeta*
giant *el gigante*
giraffe *la jirafa*
glass *el vaso*
glove *el guante*
glove puppet *el títere*
goggles *los anteojos*
go-kart *el gokart*
goldfish *el pez de colores*
golf *el golf*
goose *la oca*
gooseberry *la uva espina*
gorilla *el gorila*
grandfather *el abuelo*
grandmother *la abuela*
grapefruit *el pomelo*
grapes *las uvas*
grass *la césped*
grasshopper *el saltamontes*
great aunt *la bistía*
great grandfather *el bisabuelo*
great grandmother *la bisabuela*
great uncle *el bistío*
green *verde*
grey *gris*
guinea pig *el conejo de indias*
guitar *la guitarra*
gull *la gaviota*
gymnastics *la gimnasia*

h

hair *el pelo*
hairbrush *el cepillo*
hamburger *la hamburguesa*
hammer *el martillo*
hamper *el cesto*
hamster *el hámster*
hand fork *la horca del mano*
hand *la mano*
handbag *el bolso*
handkerchief *el panuelo*
hangar *el hangar*
hanging basket *la cesta de plantas*
happy *contento*
harp *la harpa*
hat *el sombrero*
head *la cabeza*
heart *la corazón*
heat *el calor*
heavy *pesado*
hedge *el seto*
height chart *la tabla de estatura*
helicopter *el helicoptero*
hen *la gallina*
herbs *las hierbas*
hi-fi *el estéreo*
high chair *la silla alta*
high jump *la salta alta*
hill *la colina*
hippopotamus *el hipopótamo*
hoe *la azada*
honey *la miel*
hook *el gancho*
hoop *el arco*
hooter *la sirena*
hopping *saltar*
horse *el caballo*
hose *la manga*
hot-air balloon *el globo*
hotdog *el perrito caliente*

hummingbird *el colibrí*
hundred *cien*
hutch *la conejera*

I

ice *el helado*
ice cream *el helado*
ice skates *los botes del patinaje*
ice skating *el patinaje*
iced lolly *el helado*
icicles *los carámbanos*
inside *dentro*
iris *el lirio*
iron *la plancha*
island *la isla*

j

jacket *la chaqueta*
Jack-in-the-box *la caja sorpresa*
jamjars *los tarros*
jeans *los vaqueros*
jellyfish *la medusa*
jetty *el embarcadero*
jogger *el corredor*
judo *el judo*
jug *el jarro*
juggernaut *el camión*
juice *el zumo*
jumper *el suéter*
jumping *saltar*

k

kangaroo *el canguro*
kennel *la casa del perro*
kettle *el calentador de agua*
keyboard *el teclado de música*
keyhole *el agujero de llave*
keys *las llaves*

kicking *dar un puntapié*
king *el rey*
kingfisher *el martín pescador*
kite *la cometa*
kitten *el gatito*
kiwi *el kiwi*
knee pads *la rodillera*
knee *la rodilla*
knife *el cuchillo*
knight *el caballero*
koala *la coala*

l

label *la etiqueta*
ladder *la escalera*
ladybird *la mariquita*
lake *el lago*
lamb *la oveja*
lamp *la lámpara*
lance *la lanza*
lawnmower *el cortacesped*
lead *la traílla*
leaves *los hojas*
leek *los puerros*
leg *la pierna*
lemon *el limón*
leopard *el leopardo*
lettuce *la lechuga*
life buoy *la guindola*
life vest *el chaleco salvavidas*
lift *el ascensor*
light bulb *la bombilla*
light *la luz*
light (weight) *ligero*
lighthouse *el faro*
lightning *el relámpago*
lily *la azucena*
lime *la lima*
liner *el transatlántico*
lion *el león*
lips *los labios*
litter bin *la papelera*
little *pequeño*
lizard *la lagatija*

lobster *la langosta*
lobster pot *la langostera*
log *los troncos*
lollipop *el pirulí*
lunch box *la caja de comida*

m

magazine *la revista*
magician *el mágico*
mallet *el mazo*
mango *el mango*
map *el mapa*
maracas *las maracas*
marbles *las carnicas*
mask *la máscara*
mast *el mástil*
mattress *el colchón*
meadow *el campo*
measuring tape *el metro*
medicine *la medicina*
melon *la sandía*
mermaid *la sirena*
message in a bottle *el mensaje de botella*
microwave *la micro-onda*
milk *la leche*
milkshake *el batido*
millipede *el milpiés*
mirror *el espejo*
mittens *los guantes*
mixing bowl *la escudilla*
mobile *el pendiente*
modelling clay *la arcilla*
money *el dinero*
money box *la hucha*
monkey *el mono*
mop *el fregasuelos*
moth *la mariposa nocturna*
mother *la madre*
motor boat *el barco de motor*

motorbike *la moto*
mountain *la montaña*
mouse *la rata*
mouth *la boca*
muffin *el pastel*
mug *la taza*
mushrooms *los champiñones*
music *la música*
music stand *el atril*

n

nail brush *el cepillo*
nails *los clavos*
napkin *la servilleta*
nappy *el pañal*
navy *azul oscurro*
nest *el nido*
nesting box *el nido*
new *nuevo*
newspaper *el periódico*
nightie *el camisón*
nine *nueve*
nineteen *diecinueve*

Noah's ark *la Arca de Noé*
nose *la nariz*
notes *las notas*
nurse *la enfermera*
nuts *las nueces*

o

oboe *el oboe*
octopus *el pulpo*
off (lamp) *apagado*
old *viejo*
omelette *la tortilla*
on (lamp) *puesto*
one *uno (una)*
onion *la cebolla*
open *abierto*
orange (colour) *naranja*
orange (fruit) *la naránja*
ostrich *el avestruz*

outside *fuera*
oval *la ovalada*
oven *la cocina eléctrica*
owl *el búho*
oyster *la ostra*

p

paddles *el canalete*
page boy *el paje*
paint *el bote de pintura*
paintbox *las pinturas*
paintbrush *el pincel*
painting *el dibujo*
palm *la palma*
palm tree *la palmera*
panda *el panda*
pansy *el pensamiento*
pants *las bragas*
papaya *la papya*
paper *el papel*
paper cup *la taza de papel*
parachute *el paracaída*
parcel *el paquete*
parrot *el loro*
parsnip *la chirivía*
party bag *el bolsito de fiesta*
party dress *el vestido*
party hat *el sombrero de fiesta*
path *la senda*
pavement *la acera*
paw *la pata*
peach *el melocotón*
peacock *el pavoreal*
pear *la pera*
pearl *la perla*
peas *los guisantes*
pebbles *las pierdrecitas*
pedal car *el coche*
pelican *el pelícano*
penguin *el pingüino*
penknife *la navaja*

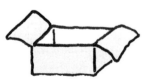

pepper *el pimiento*

personal stereo *el estéreo personal*

photograph *la foto*

piano *el piano*

pick-up truck *el camión de averías*

picnic *el picnic*

picture *la obra*

picture frame *el cuadro*

pie *la tarta*

pig *el cerdo*

pigeon *la paloma*

piggy bank *la hucha*

piglet *el cerdito*

pillow *la almohada*

pilot *el piloto*

pin board *el tablón de anuncios*

pineapple *la piña*

pink *rosa*

pipe *el caño*

pirate *el pirata*

pirate flag *la bandera de pirata*

pistol *la pistola*

pizza *la pizza*

plank *el tablón*

plaster *la tirita*

plaster cast *la escayola*

plate *el plato*

play house *la casa de muñecas*

pliers *los alicates*

plum *la ciruela*

pocket *el bolsillo*

polar bear *el oso blanco*

pole vaulting *el salto con pértiga*

pond *el estanque*

poppy *la amapola*

porcupine *el puerco espín*

porter *el portero*

porthole *la portilla*

portrait *el dibujo*

poster *el póster*

pot plant *la planta*

potato *la patata*

potty *el orinal*

pram *el cochecito*

present *el regalo*

prince *el príncipe*

princess *la princesa*

proud *orgulloso*

puddles *los charcos*

puffin *el frailecillo*

pull-along toy *la jugueta de bébés*

pulling *tirar*

pumpkin *la calabaza*

pupil *el alumno*

puppy *el cachorro*

purple *violeta*

purse *el monedero*

pushing *empujar*

puzzle *el rompecabezas*

pyjamas *el pijama*

q

queen *la reina*

queue *la cola*

r

rabbit *el conejo*

raccoon *el mapache*

racing car *el coche de carreras*

radio *la radio*

radishes *el rabaño*

railings *la verja*

railway track *la vía*

rain *la lluvia*

rainbow *el arco de iris*

rake *el rastrillo*

raspberry *la frambuesa*

rattle *el sonajero*

reading *leer*

recorder *la flauta de pico*

rectangle *el rectangulo*

red *rojo*

red pepper *el pimiento rojo*

redcurrants *la grosella roja*

refuse truck *el furgón de basura*

remote control *el tele control*

removal van *el furgón*

rhinoceros *el rhinoceronte*

rhubarb *el ruibarbo*

ribbon *la cinta*

rice *el arroz*

riding (a bicycle) *montar la bicicleta*

river *el río*

road *la calle*

robot *el robot*

rocket *el cohete*

rocking chair *la mecedora*

rocking horse *el caballo de balancín*

rocks *las rocas*

roller skating *el patinaje de ruedas*

rollerskates *los patines*

rolling pin *el rodillo de cocina*

roof *el tejado*

roof tile *la teja*

rope *la cuerda*

rose *la rosa*

rowing *el piragüismo*

rowing boat *el bote de remos*

rubber duck *el pato*

rubber ring *el aro de goma*

rucksack *la mochila*

rug *la alfombra*

ruler *la regla*

runner beans *las judías verdes*

running *correr*

runway *la pista de aterrizaje*

s

sack race *la carrera de bolsas*

sad *triste*

safety helmet *el casco*

salad *la ensalada*

salt *la sal*

sand *la arena*

sandcastle *el castillo de arena*

sandpaper *el papel de lija*

sandpit *el hoyo de arena*

sandwiches *los bocadillos*

saucepan *la cacerola*

saucer *el platillo*

sauce *la salsa*

sausage *la salchicha*

saw *la sierra*

saxophone *el saxafón*

scales *la balanza*

scarecrow *el espanta pájaros*

scarf *la bufanda*

school *el colegio*

schoolbag *el bolso*

scissors *las tijeras*

scooter *el patinete*

screwdriver *el destornillador*

screws *los tornillos*

sea *el mar*

sea shell *la concha de mar*

seahorse *el caballito de mar*

seaweed *las algas*

second *segundo*

security light *la luz de seguridad*

seeds *las semillas*

seesaw *el subibaja*

seven *siete*

seventeen *diecisiete*

sewing machine *la máquina de coser*
shampoo *el champú*
shark *el tiburón*
shawl *el chal*
shears *las tijeras de jardín*
shed *el cobertizo*
sheep *la cordera*
sheet *la sabana*
shelf *el estante*
shield *el escudo*
shirt *la camisa*
shoe shop *la zapatería*
shoes *los zapatos*
shop assistant *la dependienta*
shopper *el comprador*
shopping bag *la bolsa*
shopping trolley *el carro*
short *bajo*
shorts *los pantalones cortes*
shoulder *el hombro*
shower *la ducha*
shower curtain *la cortina de ducha*
shut *cerrado*
shy *tímido*
sign *el signo*
singing *cantar*
sink *el fregadero*
sister *la hermana*
sitting *sentar*
six *seis*
sixteen *dieciseis*
skates *los botes del patinaje*
skateboard *el mono patín*
skipping *saltar*
skipping rope *la cuerda de saltar*
skirt *la falda*
skis *el patín*
skittles *el juego de bolos*

skylight *el tragaluz*
sledge *el trineo*
sleeping *dormir*
sleeping bag *el saco de dormir*
sleepsuit *la camiseta de dormir*
slice of cake *la ración de la tarta*
slide *el tobogán*
sling *el cabestrillo*
slippers *las zapatillas*
slow *lento*
slug *la babosa*
snail *el caracol*
snake *la serpiente*
snow *la nieve*
snowflake *el copo de nieve*
snowman *el hombre de nieve*
soap *el jabón*
soccer *el fútbol*
socks *los calcetines*
sofa *el sofá*
soil *la tierra*
soldiers *los solditos*
soother *el chupete*
sorry *arrepentido*
soup *la sopa*
spade *la pala*
spaghetti *los espaguetis*
spanner *la llave de tuercas*
spider *la araña*
spider's web *la telaraña*
sponge *la esponja*
spoon *la cucharilla*
spots *los puntos*
spring *la primervera*
square *el cuadro*
squirrel *la ardilla*
stacking cups *las tazitas*
standing *esperar*
star *la estrella*
starfish *la estrella de mar*

steamroller *la apisonadora*
stethoscope *el estetoscopio*
stewardess *la azafata*
stick insect *el insecto de palo*
stool *el taburete*
storage jar *el tarro*
stork *la cigüeña*
strawberry *la fresa*
streamer *la guirnalda de papel*
street light *la farola*
street sign *el poste indicador*
stripes *las rayas*
submarine *el submarino*
sugar *el azúcar*
suitcase *la maleta*
summer *el verano*
sun *el sol*
sun hat *el sombrero de paja*
sun cream *la crema bronceadora*
sunflower *la girasol*
sunglasses *las gafas de sol*
sunshade *la sombrilla*
sunshine *el sol*
swallow *la golondrina*
swan *el cisne*
sweet potato *la batata*
sweet shop *la bombonería*
sweetcorn *la maíz*
sweets *los caramelos*
swimmer *el nadador*
swimming *la natación*
swimming trunks *el traje de baño*
swimsuit *el bañador*
swing *los columpios*
sword *la espada*
syringe *la jeringa*

†

table *la mesa*
tablecloth *el mantel*
tablemat *el salvamanteles*
tall *alto*
tambourine *la pandereta*
tandem *el tándem*
tangerine *la mandarina*
tanker *el camión de gasolina*
tap *el grifo*
tarantula *la tarántula*
tea set *el servicio de té*
tea towel *el trapo de cocina*
teacher *la profesora*
team *el equipo*
teaspoon *la cucharilla*
teddy bear *el osito*
teething ring *el chupador*
telephone *el teléfono*
television *la televisión*
temperature chart *la tabla de temperatura*
ten *diez*
tennis *el tenis*
tent *las tiendas de campaña*
thermometer *el termómetro*
thin *delgado*
third *tecero*
thirteen *trece*
thoughtful *pensativo*
three *tres*
three-legged race *la carrera de tres piernas*
thumb *el pulgar*
tickets *los billetes*
tie *la corbata*
tiger *el tigre*

tights *las medias*
till *la caja*
till receipt *el recibo*
timpani *los tímpanos*
tissues *el tisú*
toadstool *el hongo*
toaster *el tostador*
toe *el dedo de pie*
toilet *el váter*
toilet paper *el papel higiénico*
toilets *los servicios*
tomato *el tomate*
tool box *la caja de herramientas*
toothbrush *el cepillo de dientes*
toothpaste *la pasta de dientes*
top (toy) *la peonza*
top (position) *arriba*
top hat *el sombrero de copa*
torch *la lámpara de bolsillo*
tornado *el tornado*
tortoise *la tortuga*
toucan *el tucán*
towel *la toalla*
toy boat *el barco*
toy box *el baúl*
tractor *el tractór*
trainer cup *la tazita*
trainers *las zapatillas de deporte*
trampolining *el salto de trampolín*
trapdoor *la escotilla*
tray *la bandeja*
treasure chest *el cajón*
treasure map *la mapa*
tree *el árbol*
trellis *la espaldera*
triangle (instrument) *el tríangulo*

triangle (shape) *el triangulo*
tricycle *el triciclo*
trolley *la caretilla*
trombone *el trombón*
trophy *la copa*
trousers *los pantalones*
trowel *la paleta*
truck *la furgoneta*
trumpet *la trompeta*
trunk *el tronco*
T-shirt *la camiseta*
tummy *el estómago*
turkey *el pavo*
turnip *el nabo*
turtle *la tortuga marina*
twelve *doce*
twenty *veinte*
twins *los gemelos*
two *dos*

u

uncle *el tío*
up *arriba*

v

vacuum cleaner *el aspirador*
vase *el vaso de flores*
vegetables *los legumbres*
vest *la camiseta*
video *el vídeo*
village *el pueblo*
vintage car *el coche clásico*
violin *el violín*
visitor *el visitante*
vulture *el buitre*

w

waistcoat *el chaleco*

walker *el paseante*
walking *andar*
walking frame *las muletas*
walking stick *el bastón*
wall tiles *los azulejos*
wallpaper *el papel de paredes*
wand *la varilla de virtudes*
wardrobe *el armario*
washbasin *el lavabo*
washing *lavarse*
washing-up liquid *el jabón de fregar*
wasp *la avispa*
wastepaper bin *la papelera*
watch *el reloj*
water glass *el vaso de agua*
water bowl *el tazón de agua*
water jug *el cántarro*
water pot *el tarro de agua*
waterfall *la cascada*
watering can *la regadera*
water-skier *el esquiador acuatico*
waves *las olas*
waving *agitar el brazo*
weightlifting *el levantamiento de pesos*
wetsuit *el traje de baño*
whale *la ballena*
wheelbarrow *la carretilla*
wheelchair *la silla de ruedas*
wheels *las ruedas*

white *blanco*
wind *el viento*
window *la ventana*
window box *la jardinera de ventana*
windsock *la mango*
wing *el ala*
winter *el invierno*
wire basket *la cesta*
wishing well *el fuente de deseos*
wolf *el cobo*
wooden bricks *los cubos*
wooden spoon *la cuchara de palo*
workbench *la mesa de trabajo*
worktop *la tabla*
worm *el gusano*
wrapping paper *el papel*
wrist *la muñeca*
writing *escribir*

x

xylophone *el xilofón*

y

yacht *el barco de yate*
yellow *amarillo*
yoghurt *el yogur*
yo-yo *el yoyo*

z

zebra *la cebra*
zigzags *los zig zag*